Before You Begin

To be a disciple of Jesus means to follow Him. It means beco[ming like Him. When Jesus called the] twelve disciples, they left everything and followed Him on the r[oad. They stayed with Him. They] went where He went. They ate what He ate. They did what He did. The disciples wanted to be where Jesus was.

Is that your desire?

The only goal of these workbooks is to encourage believers to read their Bibles daily and process what they read. I believe that the written word of God speaks for itself. I believe that, in the written word of God, we meet the Living Word. We meet Jesus.

It is my hope that, by reading the word of God each day, you will grow close to Jesus. It is my hope that you will be His disciple, follow Him on the road, and become like Him. It is my hope that you will live your life in His presence.

One thing I ask from the LORD, this only do I seek:
that I may dwell in the house of the LORD all the days of my life,
to gaze on the beauty of the LORD and to seek him in his temple.
Psalm 27:4

Benefits of Daily Bible Reading

Increasing faith (Romans 10:17)	Renewing of the mind (Romans 12:2)
Imparting wisdom (Colossians 3:16)	Learning who you are (James 1:23-25)
Breaking of inner barriers (Jeremiah 23:29)	Modeling spiritual discipline (Deuteronomy 6:4-8)
Learning Who God is (Isaiah 55:8-11)	Equipping you for life's journey (Psalm 37:31)
Bringing peace (John 16:33)	Development and growth (Psalm 19:7-11)

How to Use this Workbook:

Get Ready
- Find a quiet place.
- Spend a few moments in prayer. Ask God to accomplish His will in you through the reading of His Word. You will write a prayer in the first journal entry. Using that prayer would be a good way to begin each session.

Read
- Read the key verse.
- Read the "Today's Reading" verses.
- Read the key verse once more, or as many times as you need to, and fully process the words.

Write
- Write your thoughts on the prompt questions or on anything that the Lord speaks to you.
- Write and draw freely. There are no wrong answers.

Pray
- Ask the Lord to continue to speak to you throughout the day.

Copyright © 2022 by Sue Dewan
All rights reserved, including the right to reproduce this book or any portion thereof in any form.
Designed by Mandy Sykes - www.mandysykes.us

Today's Reading:

Numbers 13:17-33

Numbers 14:8-9

> "If the Lord is pleased with us, he will lead us into that land, a land flowing with milk and honey, and will give it to us. Only do not rebel against the Lord."

God told them He would lead them. He told them He would do it. How many miracles had they seen? Yet ... once more they had come up against something that "couldn't be done." The Israelites had arrived at the border of the Promised Land. When they saw the enemies that would have to be defeated so they could inherit the land, they had a meltdown. They complained against God and discussed heading back to their slavery in Egypt. Joshua and Caleb were the only ones with faith that God would do what God had always done. They had seen the mighty works of God and they believed He would continue to do miracles. The multitude of others, for some reason, reacted with unbelief.

God had led them by the hand. Miracles had abounded. There were plagues in Egypt that affected everyone except the Israelites. The Red Sea parted. A pillar of fire and cloud led them. Bitter water was made sweet. Manna fell from heaven. Water gushed from a rock. Quail appeared from nowhere. God did miracle after miracle .... but the Israelites still trembled in fear every time they encountered an obstacle. "Sure," they apparently thought, "God did that in the past. How do we know He can do it again? How do we know He will?" They hadn't learned to trust in the character of God. They didn't know Him.

Do I? Do I trust Him? Father God never changes. His children can trust His word. His promises are sure (Numbers 23:19; 2 Corinthians 1:20; 2 Peter 3:9). If He says He will do something ... He will do it. If He makes a promise ... He will carry it to completion. He always keeps His promises. "Every good and perfect gift is from above, coming down from the Father of the heavenly lights, who does not change like shifting shadows" (James 1:17).

Write out a prayer asking God to help you hear Him properly. Use this prayer daily while you work through this book.

example: Dear Lord, please provide me an open mind to receive your word and a grateful heart to accept it.

What promises has God given you? Are there any that are hard to trust Him for?

example: He has promised to provide for me, but it is hard not to worry about that.

Tell Him. Write it out. Keep God's promise to you in your mind today and ask Him ... keep asking Him ... to help you stand on it.

Don't forget your prayer.

Mark 4:39

Today's Reading: Mark 4:35-41

> "He got up, rebuked the wind and said to the waves, 'Quiet! Be still!' Then the wind died down and it was completely calm."

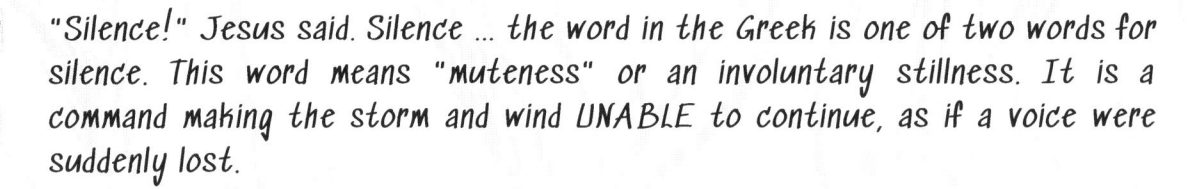

"Silence!" Jesus said. Silence ... the word in the Greek is one of two words for silence. This word means "muteness" or an involuntary stillness. It is a command making the storm and wind UNABLE to continue, as if a voice were suddenly lost.

"Be still!" Jesus also said. This word comes from the word "muzzle," and means to put a muzzle on something, to make it be silent.

Wow.

So basically, by the power of His word, Jesus muzzled the storm, making it mute and powerless.

No wonder the disciples were terrified. Jesus commanded nature to shut up ... and it did.

Jesus ... I turn over the storms in my life to You right now. The disciples thought that the storm would drown them, but Someone greater than the storm was with them.

Jesus ... You are still greater than the storm ... and You are with me (1 John 4:4).

What storms in seem so overpowering you think you might drown in them?

_____
_____
_____
_____

What would you like the Lord to do to calm your storm?

_____
_____
_____
_____

Write Jesus a note. Ask Him to be in your boat with you and to deal with the storm.

_____
_____
_____
_____
_____
_____

Don't forget your prayer.

Today's Reading:
Numbers 14:1-4

Numbers 14:2

> **All the Israelites grumbled against Moses and Aaron ...**

The Israelites sometimes forgot that God Himself was their true leader. When they got frustrated, they would attack their earthly leaders. Sometimes they remembered God, but they abandoned Him plenty of times too.

Any leader is going to tick me off sometimes. I don't like it when I don't get my way. Who does?

In the first town where we pastored a church, we were aware of another church in town that went through pastor after pastor. They had the type of leadership where they did a search and hired the pastor.

We met one of their pastors at the ministerial association. As soon as a pastor tried to get them to move forward ... they would fire him. We served in that town four years before we were transferred, and that church hired and fired three pastors within that time.

Godly leadership will sometimes "step on my toes" and point out where I can do better. Godly leadership will encourage me to grow, to change, to work, and to move out in ministry. Godly leadership will make me get out of my comfort zone. Would I rather grow? Or would I rather things stay just exactly the way they are and never change?

Nobody likes to be uncomfortable, but can it sometimes be a good thing?

_____
_____
_____
_____
_____

Have you ever resisted growing? Why?

_____
_____
_____
_____
_____

Is there any area in your life right now where growth or change is needed?

_____
_____
_____
_____
_____

Write down the names of people who might be willing to hold you accountable (and who you would listen to).

_____
_____
_____

Pray about your list of people and ask God to open up a conversation between you and one of them.

Don't forget your prayer.

Today's Reading: Mark 4:26-29

Mark 4:28

> **All by itself the soil produces grain – first the stalk, then the head, then the full kernel in the head.**

A good farmer knows how to plant and nourish and harvest. The farmer knows the field and the crop and knows about weather and seasons.

Scientists understand biology. They know how life is born, how it grows, and how it dies.

But really ... life itself is a mystery. Nobody fully understands how and why plants grow. How do water, sunshine, good soil, weeding, photosynthesis, and time ... all work together to bring about the miracle of a beautiful and fruitful plant? Why do some plants grow but not others? Why is it that one plant is lush and healthy, while one right next to it in the same soil and in the same sunlight is stunted and unhealthy ... or just dies?

That's us. We don't really understand how to bring about growth in the hearts of people. We just keep on being faithful ... planting, watering, weeding, obeying the Lord. We have no idea which ones of our actions really help grow the Kingdom of God. That's why we have to keep being obedient to the Holy Spirit. He knows (John 16:8). We don't see inside people's hearts and minds. He does. He knows. He's the one that makes it all work.

Any time I think I am smart enough to change someone, and that it is my words or actions that make the difference ... I'd better look out. I'm about to make mistakes.

Think of some times you thought you knew what was best for someone else.

_____
_____
_____
_____

Did you say or do something?

_____
_____
_____
_____

How did that turn out?

_____
_____
_____
_____

Why is it so hard to know what is best for another person?

_____
_____
_____
_____

Mark 5:41

Don't forget your prayer.

8
Today's Reading:
Mark 5:35-43

> "I say to you, GET UP!"

The ones who laughed when Jesus said the little girl was only sleeping .... how did they respond when they saw her up and around ... walking, playing, eating, hugging her parents?

The mourners' emotions underwent a radical change in just a few moments. Even if they were hired professional mourners, they must have felt some sadness at the death of a child. Then Jesus came and they were laughing in ridicule at the idea that a dead child ... well ... wasn't dead.

Then ... she wasn't dead.

Really. Not dead.

That's a lot for someone to process. What was it like for that little girl? Presumably she would live among those people the rest of her life. What was that like?

No matter where she went, everyone in town would say, "Remember when you were dead? And then you weren't? Tell us again what that was like!" She was a walking, talking, breathing testimony about Jesus and what He can do for anyone!

I too am a testimony for what Jesus does ... and can do. I was dead, but now I live. Let me tell you what that was like!

What is your testimony? What was it like ... being dead?

_____
_____
_____
_____
_____

What is it like now ... being alive in Christ?

_____
_____
_____
_____
_____

What did He do inside you?

_____
_____
_____
_____
_____

Write that out in four or five sentences as a testimony you can remember easily and share with someone else.

_____
_____
_____
_____
_____

Don't forget your prayer.

Today's Reading:
Mark 6:53-56

Mark 6:56

> **They begged Him to let them touch even the edge of His cloak, and all who touched Him were healed.**

This is Jesus' second visit to the region of Gennesaret. He is met by crowds of people. How did that happen? Jesus was from the other side of the lake ... and that's where most of His ministry had taken place. Jesus was a Jew. The region of Gennesaret was, well, pretty much everything except Jewish. He was a stranger.

The first time Jesus went to Gennesaret the residents asked Him to go away. They were unsettled when Jesus healed a demon possessed man. Then there was what happened with that herd of pigs ... (Mark 5:10-17).

So why was Jesus received so jubilantly when He returned? Remember that demon possessed man that Jesus set free? He wanted to follow Jesus, but Jesus told him, "No, go home to your family, and tell them everything the Lord has done for you and how merciful He has been" (Mark 5:19).

That man obeyed what Jesus said. He went all around telling everyone what God had done for him. He went to all ten towns of the region (Mark 5:20). I doubt very much that this man, though now sane and lucid, had time to come up with a system of beliefs. He didn't have a building ... or a program ... or a degree to tell him what to say.

I'll bet he just said to people, "Hey! Remember me? I'm that guy that used to live in the tombs and act all crazy, right? Let me tell you about Jesus. He set me free! I know, right? Can you believe it? Look! No demons!" Being a witness isn't complicated. Just tell the story.

Yesterday you wrote out a short testimony. Today you will add to it. What behaviors would people recognize about your life before Jesus?

_____
_____
_____
_____
_____
_____

What is different now?

_____
_____
_____
_____
_____

What can make you say …. "Remember what I used to be like? I'm not like that anymore! Jesus did it!" What's your story?

_____
_____
_____
_____
_____

Don't forget your prayer.

Today's Reading:

Mark 7:1-13

Isaiah 29:13

> **The Lord says:**
> **"These people come near to me with their mouth and honor me with their lips; but their hearts are far from me. Their worship of me is based on merely human rules they have been taught.**"

It is possible to look holy, to look as if you have it all together with God, and yet be (as the stories say) "far, far away." It happened during Jesus' lifetime. In fact, it may even have been common then, based on the passage from Isaiah that Jesus quoted in Mark 7.

So what does God want from me?

He wants me. He wants real. He wants me to stop pretending I am strong when I am weak. Certainly, nobody is strong when compared to Him (I Corinthians 1:27). When I know I am weak, I can go to Him to be made strong (2 Corinthians 12:9).

It's not that God doesn't want me to live a holy life. He does. But He wants it to be a authentic holy life. It has to start from inside of me and then it will show up on the outside (Mark 7:14-23). Anything else is hypocrisy.

Working with children for so many years has taught me a lot about telling the truth. A child who manipulates and lies is hard to teach. That child always has an excuse, someone else to blame, or just flat out denies bad behavior. A transparent child is easily taught. That child does something wrong and says, "I did that."

It is so much easier for God to teach me when I am transparent and real. It takes much longer if He has to get through layers of self-deceit or self-righteousness.

Okay, Lord. You see it all anyway. There is no point in trying to hide.

Write about the last time you made an excuse for yourself.

_____
_____
_____
_____
_____

Why did you do that?

_____
_____
_____
_____
_____

Write out some better ways of responding to your own imperfections.

_____
_____
_____
_____
_____
_____
_____
_____

Don't forget your prayer.

8

Today's Reading:

Mark 8:1-21

Mark 8:18

> Do you have eyes but fail to see, and ears but fail to hear? And don't you remember?

God is enough. All by Himself, He is enough for me.

When Jesus fed the five thousand, He was in Galilee, and there were twelve baskets of leftovers (Matthew 14:13-21). When He fed the four thousand, in the region of the Decapolis, there were seven baskets of leftovers. Keep those locations in mind. Why? So what?

Well, it's common knowledge that there were twelve tribes in the nation of Israel. Twelve tribes ... twelve baskets of leftovers. What about the seven baskets? According to Dr. Ray VanderLaan and Bargil Pixner (monk, Biblical scholar and archaeologist), the Talmud and the writings of the church fathers state that the people of the Decapolis belonged to the seven pagan Canaanite nations driven out of the Promised land by Joshua and the Israelites (Joshua 3:10). Seven nations ... seven baskets.

It is as if Jesus were subtly saying, "Hey, Israel, I can provide enough for your twelve tribes ... with leftovers. Hey, Decapolis, I can provide enough for your seven national identities ... with leftovers." The disciples were criticizing each other because they only had one loaf of bread to share between them. Jesus said, "Do you still not understand?" If He could multiply fish and bread for the masses, He could certainly do it for His disciples ... with leftovers.

Hey, church, hey, believers ... He can provide enough for what you need ... with leftovers.

The phrase, "You are enough," has been popular in recent years. What does that mean? Enough for what?

_____
_____
_____
_____

Is there any human who is "enough"? Why or why not?

_____
_____
_____
_____

Would you rather try to be "enough" all by yourself, or allow God to be enough within you? Why?

_____
_____
_____
_____

How will that choice affect your daily life?

_____
_____
_____
_____

Don't forget your prayer.

Mark 9:7

Today's Reading: Mark 9:2-10

> Then ... a voice came from the cloud: 'This is my Son, whom I love. Listen to him!'

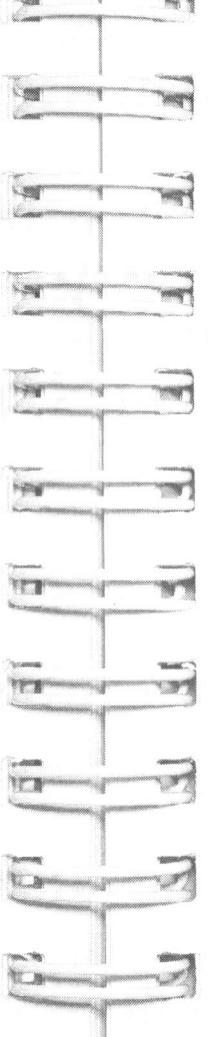

Peter and I have this in common .... when we don't know what else to do we start babbling.

They were up on a mountain, apart from everyone. Jesus was transformed. The glory of the Lord was evident. Moses and Elijah appeared from nowhere and began speaking with Jesus.

Glory of God ... Jesus ... Moses ... Elijah ... all there.

My dear friend Peter, what makes you think anyone wants to hear from you right now?

I've done that sort of thing. I've looked really stupid, too.

Thankfully, the Lord can teach me in spite of my denseness. He says to me what He said to the disciples (especially Peter). "Quit talking and listen."

When in the presence of the Lord, just be still and know that He is God (Psalm 46:10).

It is not my words people need to hear. People need to hear from Him. He really is the Son of God. If I am supposed to speak He will give me the words to say ... and it won't be babble (Luke 12:11-12).

Is it hard for you to be still and listen to God?

_____
_____
_____

Read Luke 12:11-12. Why is it important to speak the words the Holy Spirit gives you?

_____
_____
_____
_____

This may seem like a silly question with an obvious answer. Who knows more? You? Or God? (Does that make you want to draw an eye-roll emoji?)

_____
_____
_____
_____

List ways you can practice listening for the voice of the Holy Spirit.

_____
_____
_____
_____

Don't forget your prayer.

Today's Reading:
Mark 9:33-37

Mark 9:37

> **Whoever welcomes one of these little children in my name welcomes me; and whoever welcomes me does not welcome me but the one who sent me.**

To quote a line from a movie, "When you have kids, anything at all can and does happen."

Are children a bother?
Are they messy?
Do they cause a ruckus?
Sometimes ... yep ... sometimes. Maybe that is a part of the point Jesus was making.

The disciples were arguing about who among them was the greatest. Jesus drew their attention to a little child and told the disciples to be willing to be last and least. The society of that day thought of children as last and least but, the more I think about it, I wonder if Jesus was actually comparing the disciples to children. They were certainly acting like children.

Maybe the reason we are embarrassed when children behave childishly ... like children ... is because it is like looking in a mirror.
Children bicker, whine and complain.
Children don't think about consequences.
Children sulk, pout and throw a hissy fit when they don't get their way.

Maybe a part of what Jesus was saying to the disciples is, "I welcomed you with all your bad behaviors. Recognize your flaws, humble yourself, welcome each other, and welcome the least among you."

Think about the last time you saw a child behave badly. What did the child do?

_____
_____
_____
_____
_____

Do you see yourself reflected in any of that childish behavior?

_____
_____
_____
_____
_____

How does that change the way you want to interact with children?

_____
_____
_____
_____
_____
_____
_____

Don't forget your prayer.

Today's Reading:

Numbers 35:33-34

Psalms 139:14

> I praise you because I am fearfully and wonderfully made ...

Why is human life so precious?

If we are indeed just higher animals as the theory of evolution says, descended from lower primates, what does it matter? If that is the case, there are billions like us and one life doesn't matter.

If, however, we are the unique creations of an infinite God, and stamped with His image (Genesis 1:26-27), then each of us is one-of-a-kind.

There is no one else like me ... or you. There never has been and there never will be. People are not interchangeable. To destroy any person's life is to destroy the image of God woven into a priceless, never-to-be-repeated masterpiece.

Every person I meet is made in the image of God. When I serve others, I am really serving Jesus (Matthew 25:31-46). If I love God, I will love others (1 John 4:7-12).

How well am I loving my neighbors? Did I get annoyed with somebody today? That person is stamped with the image of God. Did I have some road rage? Image of God. Did I make fun of anyone in Walmart, even if just in my head? Image of God.

Did I criticize myself too much today? I'm made in the image of God too.

Who decides how much a human life is worth? Why?

_____
_____
_____
_____
_____

Think about the differences between what the world says about the value of a human life and what God says. Write about your thoughts.

_____
_____
_____
_____

You are made in the image of God. So is everyone else. How does that affect the way you want to treat yourself and others?

_____
_____
_____
_____
_____
_____
_____
_____

Don't forget your prayer.

Matthew 6:12

Today's Reading:

Mark 11:1-11

> **Forgive us our debts, as we also have forgiven our debtors.**

Forgive. It's a word that Jesus used a lot. The gospel writers used it a lot. What does it mean?

The Greek word is aphiēmi (af-ee'-ay-mee), and the literal meaning is "to send forth, cry, forgive, forsake, lay aside, leave, let alone, omit, put away, remit, suffer, or yield up" (Strong's Concordance).

Interestingly, the word is used in another way in Mark 11. Early in the chapter, the disciples went to get a donkey's colt for Jesus to ride into the city. The owners of the colt loosed (aphiēmi) the colt to them (11:6). It's the same word. They let the colt go. They surrendered control of the colt to Jesus.

There is a lot of meaning in the word forgiveness --- too much for one post --- too much for even one session of a Bible study. But this is one piece -- setting it loose -- dropping control -- letting it go.

The owners of the colt surrendered control of what was theirs to the Lord. We do the same thing when we forgive.

Do you find it easy or hard to forgive someone who hurts you?

_____
_____
_____
_____
_____

Imagine yourself as the owner of the donkey's colt. Think of handing the reins over ...just because Jesus asked you to. Can you do the same thing with your hurt?

_____
_____
_____
_____
_____

What might that look like?

_____
_____
_____
_____
_____
_____
_____
_____

Don't forget your prayer.

8

Today's Reading:

Mark 11:22-25

Mark 11:25

> **And when you stand praying, if you hold anything against anyone, forgive him, so that your Father in heaven may forgive your sins.**

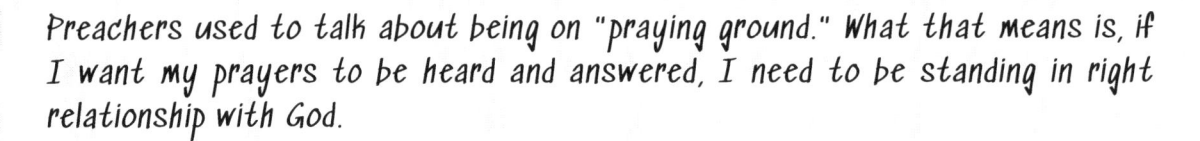

Preachers used to talk about being on "praying ground." What that means is, if I want my prayers to be heard and answered, I need to be standing in right relationship with God.

Do I have unforgiveness in my heart? My prayers won't be answered. Is there sin in my life ... unconfessed sin I am aware of? My prayers won't be answered (Psalm 66:18).

It's not that God is a big meanie, or that He doesn't love me. The truth is ... He is not a wimpy parent. I can't stamp my feet at Him and say, "If You really love me, You will give me everything I want."

My Father loves me so much that He wants what is eternally good for me. God may be trying to call my attention to a sin or a problem in my life. Unanswered prayer may be one way He gets my attention.

So .... if I find my prayers are not being answered, I will not doubt God. I will check my life and my heart. I will make sure I am standing on praying ground.

The inability to forgive in a believer's life is a really big deal to God. Why do you think that is so?

_____
_____
_____
_____

What does forgiveness look like in daily life? What does it involve?

_____
_____
_____
_____

Now look back at what you wrote and circle anything that needs work in your life. Write one way you want to put forgiveness to work in your life today.

_____
_____
_____
_____
_____
_____
_____

Don't forget your prayer.

Today's Reading:

Deuteronomy 1:5-8, 19-36

Deuteronomy 1:31

> **There you saw how the Lord your God carried you, as a father carries his son, all the way you went until you reached this place.**

It can be a good thing for me to look backwards and see where I have been wrong. If I am wise, a good review will keep me from making similar mistakes in the future.

God's grace means that I can review past sins without guilt or shame because they have been washed in the blood of the Lamb. I can remember them with gratitude for my salvation and cleansing, and for the lessons I have been taught.

In Deuteronomy 1, the new generation of Israelites is about to cross the Jordan and enter the Promised Land. Moses isn't going to be able to go with them. Joshua will be their new leader.

At God's command, Moses does a long history lesson with the Israelites. He reviews all their errors. Why? To berate them? To make them feel bad?

No.

God doesn't review the sins of the nation to make them feel bad. He does it to say ... you did that then ... don't do that now. Learn.

Be honest. Review the past to learn and be blessed for the future. Put away what needs to be put away. Don't make excuses. Don't hold on to the ugly. Let God wash it clean or wash it away.

Then go forward.

How easy is it for you to review your own sin or mistakes? Do you do that with shame and guilt? Do you look at them in the light of God's grace? All of the above?

_____
_____
_____
_____

What is a helpful way for you to look at past sins and failures? What would you like to gain from reviewing them?

_____
_____
_____
_____

Now write about one sin or failure that you HAVE learned from. How did you grow?

_____
_____
_____
_____
_____
_____

Today's Reading:
Mark 13:31-37
Deuteronomy 8:7-14

Deuteronomy 8:7,9

> **For the Lord your God is bringing you into a good land – a land with brooks, streams and deep springs gushing out into the valleys and hills ... a land where bread will not be scarce and you will lack nothing ...**

We don't know when He is coming ... but He is. We see signs and think, "Maybe now. Maybe today," but we don't know for sure.

I hope it is soon.

When the Hebrews were headed to the Promised Land, they were going to Israel. When Jesus followers think of the Promised Land, we may think of Heaven.

I would submit that Jesus followers already live in the Promised Land because we are citizens of the Kingdom of God.

I love the description in Deuteronomy 8:7-10. He has brought us to a good place, where the Water of Life is flowing, and the Bread of Life is found in abundance.

We lack nothing we need for our souls ... nothing at all ... if we abide in Him. He is our Promised Land.

I wonder what life would have been like for the Hebrews if they had loved God as much as He loved them? What would it have been like if they had said, "Promised Land? Okay, we will follow You there if that's where You want us. Or we will settle down right here where we are if You like. Any place You are ... that's where we want to be."

Lord, Your presence is my Promised Land.

Jesus is called Immanuel, "God with us" (Matthew 1:23). He is God ... with you. Write about that.

_____
_____
_____
_____

What does "home" mean to you?

_____
_____
_____
_____

When you think about God's presence being your home NOW, what is the picture in your head?

_____
_____
_____
_____
_____
_____
_____

Don't forget your prayer.

8

Today's Reading:

Mark 16:1-7

Mark 16:6

> **You are looking for Jesus the Nazarene, who was crucified. He has risen! He is not here.**

They wanted to be where Jesus was. They wanted to do what they could for Him. They needed to grieve. They needed to complete some customary rituals for the dead. It was the right thing to do.

There was a big stone in the way. They weren't strong enough to move it. There was an armed guard (Matthew 27:65-66). Would the guards help? Would they be an additional obstruction? They went anyway. They didn't know what would happen, or if they would be able to complete their task, but they went anyway ... hoping.

There is an awe-inspiring faith in the simple act of these women. Jesus had worked plenty of miracles while He lived. They had trusted Him. Could He somehow help them ... even now? Would God help them? They probably weren't really thinking ... just doing what seemed right ... and God blessed it.

They didn't have to worry about the stone. It was already rolled away by an angel (Matthew 28:2). They didn't have to worry about the guards. They were unconscious (Matthew 28:4).

They didn't complete their mission to anoint the body. Instead of finding a dead body they were on the spot to hear about the greatest event in all human history. He wasn't there. He was raised from the dead!

Go where Jesus is ... go where He is leading. Do what you can. Do the right thing. You may very well be right on time for the most amazing of miracles.

Have you ever been assigned a task that felt too big for you? What is that like?

_____

_____

_____

_____

Throughout the Bible we see countless servants of the Lord who were assigned seemingly impossible tasks. Make a list of some that you can recall.

_____

_____

_____

_____

How did God come through for those believers?

_____

_____

_____

_____

_____

_____

_____

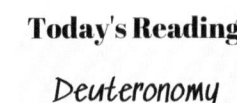

Today's Reading:

Deuteronomy 9:1-3

Don't forget your prayer.

Zechariah 4:6

> 'Not by might nor by power, but by my Spirit,' says the Lord Almighty.

The Israelites were going to the land the Lord promised them. They were following His directions. He TOLD them to go and led them on the way there.

He went before them and with them.

Now they were facing some giants.

I've been a manager before. When I gave my staff instructions, and they followed them to the letter, it was my responsibility if the plan failed. It was my responsibility to see that my staff had the training and resources to do what needed to be done. If my staff did as I instructed, and the plan still failed ... that was on me.

Father God is a much better manager than I am.

When I am walking in obedience ... it is the Father's job to make sure I can fulfill His will. He is responsible for the power and the resources (Zechariah 4:6). I am just responsible to follow His lead (Proverbs 3:5-6).

The Lord will take care of the giants ... one way or another. I will not be destroyed.

In fact ... together we will win!

Think about this phrase that was popular some years ago ... "LET GO, AND LET GOD." What does that mean?

_____
_____
_____
_____
_____

Have you ever done something just because the Lord told you to?

_____
_____
_____
_____
_____

If so ... what happened? If not ... what do you think might still happen?

_____
_____
_____
_____
_____
_____
_____

Don't forget your prayer.

Today's Reading:
Galatians 1:10 - 19

Galatians 1:10

> Am I now trying to win the approval of human beings, or of God? Or am I trying to please people? If I were still trying to please people, I would not be a servant of Christ.

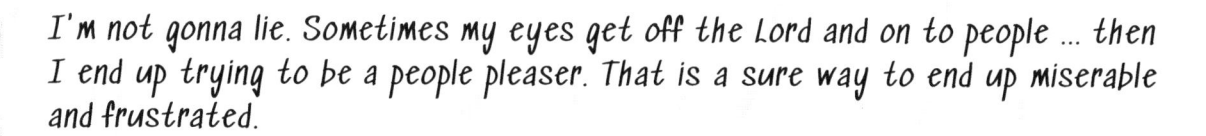

I'm not gonna lie. Sometimes my eyes get off the Lord and on to people ... then I end up trying to be a people pleaser. That is a sure way to end up miserable and frustrated.

I have lots of wonderful people in my life, but it is only my Father Who ....

... sees me completely and exactly as I am and still loves me without annoyance or impatience.
... really, truly, absolutely wants me around 24/7/365.
... always hears my heart.
... sees every little improvement (and hangs the evidence on His heavenly refrigerator).
... sees every place I need to grow.
... knows exactly how to help me grow.
... picks me up when I fall or waits for me to get up, and knows when to do which one.
... and so much more... everything I need for life and godliness (2 Peter 1:3).

So if I don't exactly do everything right by other people's standards today, I hope those who love me will let me know. Really. Then I can go talk to my Father about it and see what He says.

This may seem like a silly question, but is it possible to please everyone?

_____
_____
_____
_____

Do you try? Why or why not?

_____
_____
_____
_____

What do you think? Is it hard to please God? Is it easier than we might think?

_____
_____
_____
_____
_____
_____

Don't forget your prayer.

Today's Reading: Deuteronomy 16:1-8

Hebrews 9:28

"... so Christ was sacrificed once to take away the sins of many people; and he will appear a second time, not to bear sin, but to bring salvation to those who are waiting for him."

The Passover celebration sure sounds like a lot of effort. In fact, it sounds like all the ceremonial commands took effort to obey. I think that may very well be the point.

Perhaps the ceremonies, sacrifices and tasks were not only about the actual action, but also about the time and effort set apart. The Hebrews were required to take the time to go to a special place to celebrate. They ended up having to travel what might have been as much as a week to go all the way to Jerusalem. That is a lot of time and effort set apart and away from daily life.

The Lord wants me to stop my daily routine and set apart time with Him.

If I can't find time to set apart for the Lord, then I need to prioritize my life. I may have to reorganize, or I may have to cut something out to make space. I may just have to tell people ... the door is closed for a reason. I may have to tell people, "I'm going to weekly Bible Study because I need to. I'll do what you want at another time."

Of course, going to Jerusalem also meant that the pilgrim was in the company of other believers. The pilgrim was going where there was someone who could help get the sacrifices just right. The journey provided the opportunity for family time on the road. Sounds like a good church service to me.

What times have you set apart just so you can be where Jesus is?

_____
_____
_____
_____
_____

Do you feel that the time and effort is sufficient? Why or why not?

_____
_____
_____
_____
_____

What do you want to include most in your time set apart with the Lord?

_____
_____
_____
_____
_____
_____
_____
_____

Today's Reading:
Deuteronomy 18:9

Don't forget your prayer.

1 John 2:6

> **Whoever claims to live in him must live as Jesus did.**

"Don't imitate the nations around you," God told the Israelites. "Don't be like them or do what they do."

We tend to do that, don't we? We find someone we want to be like and imitate them, for good or ill.

Even as believers we tend to do that. We see someone we think has it all together, and we decide, "I want to be like that person."

Do we really? Do we know "that person's" life and struggles? The thoughts and battles of the heart and mind? The joys and pains?

Even Paul warned believers, "Follow me as I follow Christ" (1 Corinthians 11:1). In other words ... imitate the <u>Jesus</u> you see in me, but not anything else.

So who are we supposed to imitate?
Jesus, of course (1 John 2:6).
Follow in His footsteps (1 Peter 2:21).
Have His attitude (Philippians 2:3-8).
Serve as He served (John 13:12-15).
Love as He loved (John 13:34).
Forgive as He forgave (Ephesians 4:32).

Don't be caught dead imitating anyone else. Literally.

Have you ever imitated anyone? Even as a child? List those people. Do you want to imitate them now? Why or why not?

_____
_____
_____
_____
_____

Has imitating someone else ever lead you down the wrong path?

_____
_____
_____
_____
_____

Is there anyone you know that has a walk with Jesus you want to imitate? What is it about that person that is Christlike?

_____
_____
_____
_____
_____
_____
_____
_____

Don't forget your prayer.

Today's Reading:
Galatians 2:19-21

Galatians 2:20

> **I have been crucified with Christ and I no longer live, but Christ lives in me.**

It has never been about me. It has always been about Jesus.

When I try to be holy by myself, I fail miserably. It is too much. I don't have the ability. I will be condemned by the standard of God's holiness, goodness, and righteousness. I cannot measure up.

Thanks be to God I don't have to measure up by myself! I don't have to be good enough. Jesus is good enough for both of us.

The world tells me to keep trying. It says, "Don't quit. Never stop ... do it all yourself."

God says, "Surrender. Tap out. Cry 'uncle'! It is Christ who lives in you ... and He can do all things."

If I tried to do it all myself now, I would be saying that the sacrifice of Jesus is meaningless and accomplished nothing. I would be saying that I did not need His blood to redeem me, save me, and justify me. I'd be saying I don't need His resurrection to give me new life. How foolish would that be?

And so I say, "I am determined to know nothing ... except Christ and Him crucified" (1 Corinthians 2:2). And so I sing, "Absolutely nothing, nothing, nothing but the blood of Jesus."

Why is human goodness so miserably inadequate?

_____
_____
_____
_____
_____

Say this out loud: "I no longer live, but Christ lives in me." What does that mean for your life?

_____
_____
_____
_____
_____

Now say this out loud: "I am determined to know nothing ... except Christ and Him crucified." If you live by that statement how will it affect the way you view yourself?

_____
_____
_____
_____
_____
_____
_____
_____

Don't forget your prayer.

Romans 12:18

Today's Reading: Deuteronomy 22:1-4

> **If it is possible, as far as it depends on you, live at peace with everyone.**

God gave some very interesting laws to the Hebrews. In Exodus 23:19 and Deuteronomy 14:21, He commanded them, "Don't boil a baby goat in its mother's milk." It mattered enough for God to say it twice!

In Deuteronomy 22:6-7, He commands, "If you find a bird's nest on the ground with both mother and babies (or eggs), you can take the young, but let the mother go." With that last one there is a reward promised: "so you may prosper and have a long life."

Well ... how come? Why did God emphasize these commands? What is the point? We are not told.

Theologians have proposed a variety of reasons for the giving of these laws, but I tend to favor one. The two laws are almost the same law ... along with laws like the ones in Deuteronomy 22:1-4.

These laws can be summed up in three words: DON'T BE HEARTLESS. For real. What kind of person would cook a baby animal in its mother's milk? Who would eat that? Or maybe ... don't be so stinking selfish. Leave the momma bird so she can lay more eggs for someone else ... or even to hatch.

Help your neighbor. Don't think about it. Go do it! Yes, you can make the time. Figure it out. Don't be heartless.

Here is another interesting command: "Do not curse the deaf or put a stumbling block in front of the blind, but fear your God" (Leviticus 19:14). Can that be summed up by saying, "Thus says the Lord, 'Don't be a mean, heartless person.'"?

_____
_____
_____
_____

Why do you think commands like this are necessary?

_____
_____
_____
_____

Can you think of any other commands like this the Lord might give us for this day and time?

_____
_____
_____
_____
_____
_____
_____

Don't forget your prayer.

8

Today's Reading:

Luke 1:42-48
Galatians 3:14

Galatians 3:14

> **He redeemed us in order that the blessing given to Abraham might come to the Gentiles through Christ Jesus, so that by faith we might receive the promise of the Spirit.**

Those who take the Lord at His word are blessed. They may still receive a blessing, yes, but they are already blessed. What does that mean?

There are some who would say that being blessed means that God fulfills their wishes and gives them what they ask for. That does not seem to be the Biblical definition of blessed. How could that be so if Mary is already blessed?

At the point in her life described in Luke, Mary is in a very difficult place ... unmarried, expecting a child, and with a story to tell that many, surely, would not believe. Yet the angelic visitor calls her blessed.

So what does it mean to be blessed by God? Galatians 3:14 makes it clear that blessing from God isn't about material things, but about something far greater and more important—the promise of the Spirit. He wants to give us the blessing of Abraham, who was called a friend of God (Isaiah 41:8). Wow ... a friend of God.

The Biblical view of blessing involves a walking, talking, breathing friendship with God the Father.

If my view of blessing is limited to material things, then I am thinking as the world does and not as the Bible teaches. How much greater are the spiritual and heavenly riches God wants to bestow on me. Because I am His friend and His very presence is with me, I can be blessed in any and every circumstance (Philippians. 4:11). It truly is "Who you know."

What heavenly and spiritual blessings has the Father already bestowed on you?

_____
_____
_____
_____

How do these eternal blessings comfort and sustain you when life is difficult?

_____
_____
_____
_____

Which aspect of your friendship with God do you treasure most?

_____
_____
_____
_____
_____
_____
_____

Don't forget your prayer.

8

Today's Reading:
Deuteronomy 30:10-16

Hebrews 10:24-25

> And let us consider how we may spur one another on toward love and good deeds, not giving up meeting together, as some are in the habit of doing, but encouraging one another – and all the more as you see the Day approaching.

I can't walk this life of faith out on my own. The Lord says that the commands He gave are not too hard to follow. But I'm about to finish reading through the five books of the Law and there are a lot of instructions there. It seems complicated to me.

Then I remembered that the Law, and this statement here in Deuteronomy 30, were not given to just one person. God was speaking to a community ... and it was the whole community that was supposed to live out the commands together. He had given all the words publicly to the whole nation. They were supposed to help each other.

I can't remember everything. I don't know how to do everything. Sometimes I just don't feel like doing anything. Sometimes I fail.

When I live in fellowship with a group of other believers .... one remembers what another forgets ... there are specialists in certain areas, people who know how to do things I'm not good at ... there are people to encourage me and keep me in the path ... there are friends to help me when I fail. There are people to pray for me, to remind me of the work of the Holy Spirit in me and to help me listen to His voice (Hebrews 10:24-25).

The world is getting to be a more complicated and crazy place every day. Even if some day I find I can't be a part of a church in the traditional way, I will still need to find a way to be a part of a fellowship of Christ followers. The Lord has always intended for His followers to walk out their faith together ... in community.

What is the goal of walking out faith with a community?

_____

_____

_____

_____

It's easy to criticize churches and fellowships when they are not, perhaps, what they ought to be. Instead of criticizing, what can you do to somehow be a part of a group of believers that encourage each other?

_____

_____

_____

_____

What might you get from a fellowship like that? What might you give?

_____

_____

_____

_____

_____

_____

_____

Don't forget your prayer.

Today's Reading:
Luke 10:25-37

Galatians 5:14

> **For the entire law is fulfilled in keeping this one command: 'Love your neighbor as yourself.'**

Who is my neighbor? A man asked Jesus that question once (Luke 10:29). He might have been surprised by the answer. Jesus told the story of the good Samaritan.

A neighbor, according to the parable, may very well be anybody. It is someone I happen to meet. It is the stranger.

My neighbor is the person who hates me that I find injured on the side of the road. Why do I say that? Well, Jews and Samaritans hated each other, and the story is about a Samaritan who went out of his way to help a Jew ... a man who hated him. Jesus turned the question He was asked on its head. He answered it by asking the questioner, "Are you being a neighbor?"

I act like a neighbor when I do the Christlike thing and show compassion. I act like a neighbor when I take time out for someone in need. Who is my neighbor these days? Well ... anybody.

Am I being the neighbor Jesus called me to be? Am I Christlike to friend and stranger alike? Am I a neighbor to the person on social media that says something I disagree with? Am I a neighbor to people who hate the type of person I am? Am I a neighbor to the hurting?

The good Samaritan took great care to help someone he had no reason to help. Jesus says to me, "Go and do likewise."

Make a list of everyone who is likely to be your neighbor today.

_____
_____
_____
_____
_____

Each of those people need a different kind of compassion and love. What are some ways you can show love?

_____
_____
_____
_____
_____

The Samaritan took significant time and went to considerable expense to help his enemy. It's not always possible to do that. How can you be alert for times you CAN help more significantly?

_____
_____
_____
_____
_____
_____
_____
_____

Don't forget your prayer.

Today's Reading:
Galatians 6:1-10

Galatians 6:3

> **If anyone thinks they are something when they are not, they deceive themselves.**

In the New Living Translation, the key verse says ... "If you think you are too important to help someone, you are only fooling yourself. You are not that important" (Galatians 6:3).

God has a way of putting me in my place if I get a little too full of myself. It's never fun. Some of those times have been particularly memorable.

I remember one time I was praying. In that prayer I told God that another believer was a loser. Yeah ...

I swear that I know what silence in heaven sounds like. It felt like all the angels suddenly stopped what they were doing, turned, and looked at me in disbelief. After a pause that felt like forever, as I stood there hanging my head in shame, I heard the stern voice of my Father say, "There are no losers in my kingdom."

That was 45 years ago when I was a teenager. I haven't forgotten it. It definitely left a mark. I'm not here for myself. We are not here for ourselves.

We are here to serve the Lord ... and to encourage one another. Any time I think I am someone more special than my brothers and sisters in Christ, the Lord is going to remind me that He loves all of His children with the same great love.

"The person you love the most is that person you think about most" (Sue Dewan). Yeah. I'm quoting myself, LOL. Do you think I'm right? Why or why not?

_____
_____
_____
_____

Who do you think about most? Yourself? That would be typical. Jesus? That would be great. Other people? What do you think about that?

_____
_____
_____
_____

The title of this workbook is "Where Jesus Is." What are some ways you can encourage yourself to think more about Jesus first so that you can live in His presence?

_____
_____
_____
_____
_____

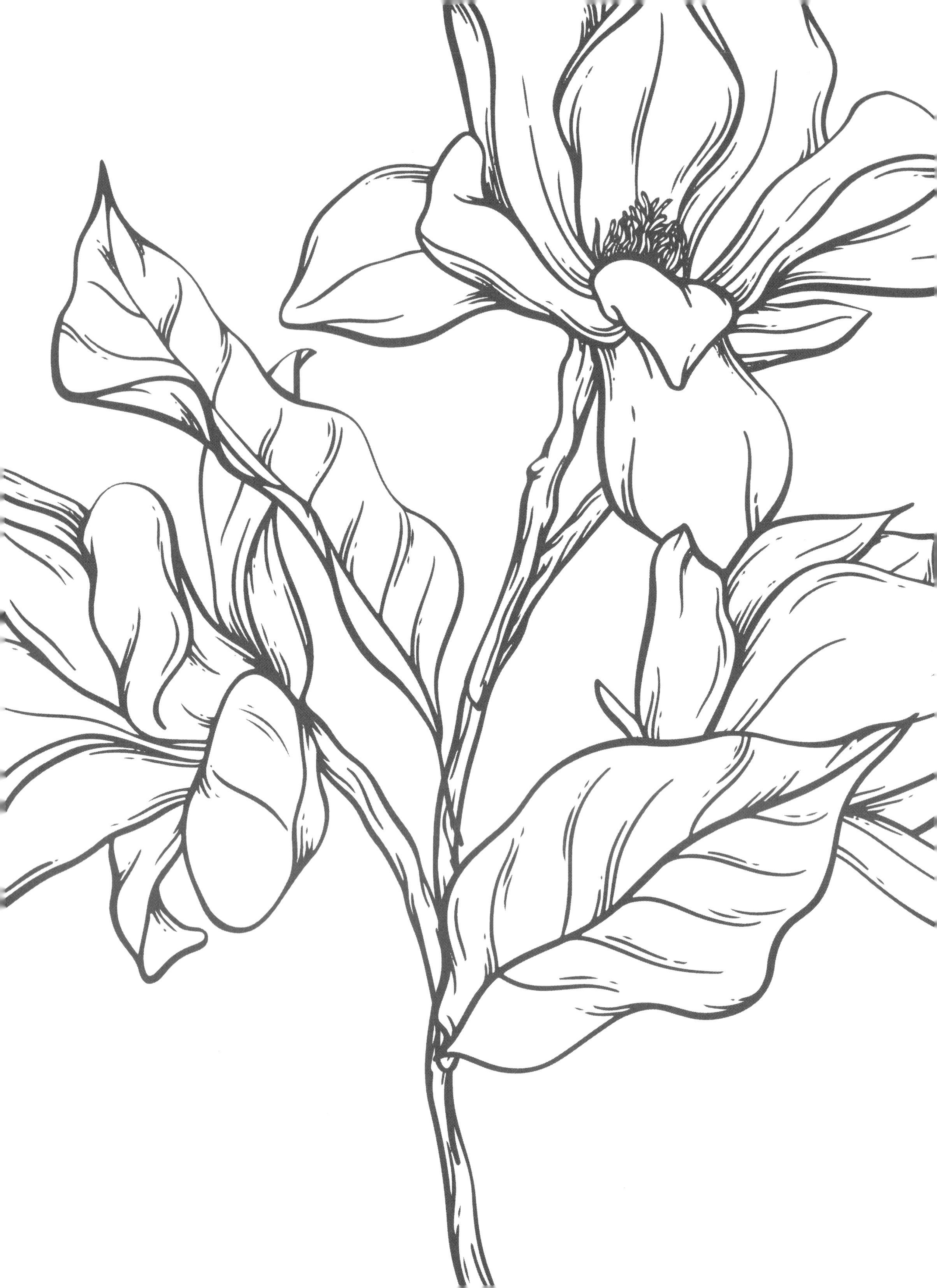

Now That You're Done!

First, let me say that I am PROUD of YOU! It isn't easy to complete something that is purely for personal growth ... especially if you only have YOURSELF to hold YOU accountable.

If you have read that paragraph before because you have done other workbooks ... I'm STILL proud of you! Keep going!

Next ... keep praying. Keep reading. Keep asking God to speak to you through His Word.

I have a private Facebook Group of people who are reading the Bible together. It is called Walking Together. The readings are not intimidating, but we do follow a yearly plan.

If you are interested, you can go to the link, ask to join, and complete the membership questions. Don't forget to mention that you have completed this workbook!

https://www.facebook.com/groups/201022248238160/

Workbooks and Journals by Sue Dewan:

The Word 101
Book #1 of The Word Series

Walking Together
Book #2 of The Word Series

Where Jesus Is
Book #3 of The Word Series

Sermon & Worship Journal
A guided journal for taking "notes" during service

You can also subscribe to receive different workbooks every month! Go to www.acpress.us/workbooks for more information.

Made in the USA
Columbia, SC
24 November 2022